How to rekind

CW00506709

A step by step guide fc

spark into your sex life. ~~~~~~~~~~, ~~~~~,

please, tease and and make him succumb

completely to you.

Joan T. Carr

Table of contents

Chapter 1: Male Sex Drive

Sex Drive and the Brain

Sex drive or desire is frequently termed as libido. Sex drive, or libido, refers to a person's urge to participate in sexual behavior. There is no quantifiable measurement for libido. Instead, sex desire is interpreted in meaningful terms. For example, a low libido denotes a diminished interest or desire in sex.

The male libido dwells in two parts of the brain: the cerebral cortex and the limbic system. These areas of the brain are important to a man's sex desire and performance. They are so vital, in fact, that a guy may have an orgasm merely by imagining or fantasizing about a sexual encounter.

The cerebral cortex is the gray matter that makes up the outer layer of the brain. It's the region of the brain that's responsible for higher activities like planning and reasoning. This involves thinking about sex. When a guy feels aroused, impulses that originate in the cerebral cortex may interact with other sections of the brain and nerves. Some of these neurons increase the pulse rate and blood flow to your genitals. They also indicate the process that causes an erection.

The limbic system encompasses various areas of the brain: the hippocampus, hypothalamus and amygdala, among others. These components are linked with emotion, motivation, and sex desire.

What is Low Libido?

Low libido denotes a diminished desire in sexual engagement. It's typical to lose interest in sex from time to time, and libido levels change during life. It's also common for your interest not to match your partner's at times. However, reduced libido for a lengthy period of time may create worry for men. It may occasionally be a sign of an underlying health concern.

Pr obable Reasons of Decreased Libido in Males;

*Low Testosterone

Testosterone is an essential male hormone. In males, it's largely generated in the testicles. Testosterone is important for growing muscles and bone mass, and for boosting sperm production. Testosterone levels can play into your sex desire. Normal testosterone levels may vary. However, adult males are deemed to have low testosterone, or low T, when their levels fall below 300 nomograms per deciliter (ng/ld.), according to standards.

When a man testosterone levels decline, the desire for sex also diminishes. Decreasing testosterone is a typical aspect of aging. However, a significant decline in testosterone might lead to diminished libido. One may be able to use supplements or gels to raise the testosterone levels.

*Medications

Taking some drugs may suppress testosterone levels, which in turn may contribute to poor libido. For example, blood pressure drugs such as ACE inhibitors and beta-blockers may hinder ejaculation and erections. Other drugs that may reduce testosterone levels include:
Chemotherapy or radiation therapies for cancer
Hormones used to treat prostate cancer
Corticosteroids
Opioid pain medications, such as morphine (MorphaBond, MS Contin) and oxycodone (OxyContin, Percocet) (OxyContin, Percocet)
An antifungal drug called ketoconazole
Cimetidine (Tagamet), which is used for heartburn and gastroesophageal reflux disease (GERD) (GERD)
Anabolic steroids, which may be taken by sportsmen to improve muscle mass
Certain antidepressants
If your man is experiencing the effects of low testosterone due to medication, talk to your doctor. They may advise you to switch medications.

*Restless Legs Syndrome (RLS)

Restless legs syndrome (RLS) is the uncontrolled need to move your legs. Research indicated that men with RLS are at greater risk for developing erectile dysfunction (ED) than those without RLS. ED happens when a guy can't get or maintain an erection. In the study, researchers observed that men who experienced RLS occurrences at least five times per month were around 50 percent more likely to acquire ED than those without RLS. Also, males who experienced RLS episodes more often were significantly more likely to become impotent.

*Depression

Depression influences many elements of a person's life. People with depression report a lessened or total loss of interest in things they formerly considered gratifying, including sex. Low libido is also a negative effect of various antidepressants, including: serotonin-norepinephrine reuptake inhibitors (SNRIs), such as duloxetine (Cymbalta) selective serotonin reuptake inhibitors (SSRIs), including fluoxetine (Prozac) and sertraline (Zoloft) (Zoloft) However, the norepinephrine and dopamine reuptake inhibitor (NRDI) bupropion (Wellbutrin SR, Wellbutrin XL) hasn't been demonstrated to lower the libido.

Talk to your doctor if your man is on antidepressants and have a reduced libido. They could address your adverse effects by modifying your dosage or having you switch to another medication.

*Chronic Sickness

When you're not feeling well due to the symptoms of a chronic health condition, such as chronic pain, sex is usually low on your list of priorities. Certain disorders, such as cancer, might affect sperm production numbers as well. Other chronic illnesses that can take a toll on your man libido include:

Type 2 diabetes

Obesity

High blood pressure

High cholesterol

Chronic lung, heart, kidney, and liver failure

*Sleep Troubles

Research indicated that nonobese males with obstructive sleep apnea (OSA) suffer reduced testosterone levels. In turn, this leads to reduced sexual activity and desire. In the study, researchers discovered that roughly one-third of the males who had severe sleep apnea also had lower levels of testosterone. The researchers observed that the effects of reducing sleep on testosterone levels were notably obvious between 2:00 pm and 10:00 pm the following day.

*Aging

Testosterone levels, which are connected to desire, are at their greatest when males are in their late teens. In their elder years, it may take longer to achieve orgasms, ejaculate, and feel aroused. Their erections may not be as hard, and it may take longer for their penis to get erect. However, drugs are available that may assist address these difficulties.

*Stress

If a man is preoccupied by events or periods of intense pressure, sexual desire may drop. This is because stress may affect hormone levels. The arteries may constrict in times of stress. This constriction inhibits blood flow and possibly causes ED.

Stress is hard to avoid. Relationship issues, approaching divorce, confronting the loss of a loved one, financial concerns, a new infant, or a hectic work environment are just few of the life situations that may dramatically alter the desire for sex. Stress management approaches, such as breathing exercises, meditation, and talking to a therapist, may assist.

*Low Self-esteem

Self-esteem is described as the overall opinion a person has about their own self. Low self-esteem, low confidence, and poor body image can take a toll on emotional health and well-being. If feeling undesirable, it'll likely put a damper on sexual encounters. Not like what is seen in the mirror might even make one want to avoid having sex entirely.

Low self-esteem may also generate concern about sexual performance, which may lead to difficulties with ED and diminished sexual desire.

Over time, self-esteem concerns may develop in broader mental health problems, such as depression, anxiety, and drug or alcohol misuse, all of which have been associated with reduced libido.

*Too Little (or too much) Exercise

Too little or too much exercise may also be responsible for reduced sex desire in men... Too little exercise (or none at all) may lead to a variety of health concerns that might impact sexual desire and pleasure. Getting regular exercise may lessen the risk for chronic illnesses such as obesity, high blood pressure, and type 2 diabetes, all of which are connected with reduced libido. Moderate exercise is known to decrease cortisol levels at night and reduce stress, which may assist improve sex desire.

On the other side, over-exercising has also been demonstrated to harm sexual health. Higher levels of chronic intensive and extended endurance training on a regular basis were highly related with reduced libido ratings in males.

*Alcohol

Heavy alcohol intake, or more than 14 mixed drinks in a week, has also been associated with a drop in testosterone production. Over a lengthy period of time, large doses of alcohol might impair male sex desire. It is proposed that an average adult man should consume two or less alcoholic beverages every day; any more than this may contribute to long-term health problems.

*Drug Usage

In addition to alcohol, the use of cigarettes, marijuana, and illegal substances such as opiates has also been related to a reduction in testosterone production. This might result in a loss of sexual desire. Smoking has also been demonstrated to have a deleterious influence on sperm production and sperm mobility.

Physical and Emotional Negative Consequences of Decreased Libido

A diminished sex desire may be highly upsetting for a man. Low libido may lead to a vicious cycle of physical and mental side effects, including ED(erectile dysfunction), which is the inability to sustain an erection long enough to enjoy pleasurable sex.
ED may lead a guy to develop anxiety surrounding sex. This can lead to tension and conflicts between him and his partner, which may in turn lead to fewer sexual encounters and more relationship issues. Failure to perform because of ED may generate emotions of sadness, self-esteem difficulties, and poor body image.

When to be Worried?

Anonymous(Question)
Since it's usual for libido to vary from time to time, when (at what time length) is low libido a reason for concern?
Anonymous (Answer)
The definition of low libido depends on the person experiencing the low libido, that is, it must be compared to what is considered that

person's normal libido. However, if someone notes issues with libido without a clear stimulus for several weeks, it is reasonable to discuss the problem with a physician, who may be able to determine if an underlying physiologic or psychological issue is causing these concerns.

How to Increase Male Sex Drive

The following methods helps to improve sex drive for your man;

*Sex Therapy

A sex therapist may aid with sexual difficulties. While they may assist improve sex desire, they can also encourage individuals to attain orgasm.

*Increase Sleep

A research indicated that greater sleep duration in males related to a higher degree of next-day sexual desire.

*Aphrodisiacs

Herbal aphrodisiac such as yohimbine and Eurycoma longifolia, may aid to improve male sex desire. Certain foods like strawberries, chocolate, and raw oysters might potentially have aphrodisiac effects.

*Exercise

People may boost their libido with exercise, mindfulness, and yoga.

*Testosterone Treatment

Testosterone treatment in elderly guys has demonstrated it might help them restore sexual drive.

*Nutritional Food

Following a nutritious diet can benefit people's sex drive by promoting good circulation and heart health and removing specific foods that can decrease libido.

For circulation and stamina; keeping the circulatory system in good working order is essential for sexual health. Better circulation can lead to an improved sexual response in men. This is especially true for the erectile response. Cardiac health is also crucial for stamina. In other words, if it is good for the heart, it is good for a person's sex life.

Some recommended diet includes;

A wide range of fruits and vegetables

Whole grains and plenty of fiber

Healthful oils, such as olive oil and sunflower oil

Seafood, nuts, and legumes

Research suggests that following this heart-healthy diet can improve certain aspects of sexual health.

Chapter 2 : How to Arouse him Emotionally

In order for both mates to be involved in a relationship, there needs to be an emotional connection afoot. For women it is simple to figure out what they need for a good emotional connection: physical contact, engaging discussion, comfort, caring, support. But when it comes to finding out how to connect with your man on an emotional level, it may be a bit of a mind scratcher.

Women are often more willing to connect with their partner and spend their time and energy, whilst men are more inclined to lie back and observe how the entire thing plays out. Connecting with your man on an emotional level is typically what drives him to fall in love with you. This is what converts one sinful night into a lifetime of bliss. The trick is learning how to do it.

Here are the finest tips on how to connect with your man on an emotional level:

So, how can you connect with a guy emotionally? No matter whether you've been together 10 days or 10 years, sustaining emotional connection is the thing that is going to keep you guys together for a lifetime. If you're seeking to develop or recreate a relationship with your spouse you have to concentrate on his needs. Creating an emotional connection is all about interacting and connecting in a manner that excites him, not you.

1. Keep it Sexy

It's no secret that males adore sex. Not just because it feels wonderful, but because it raises his ego, helps him view you in a sensuous and strong light, and it makes him feel a connection to you. While the idea that men desire sex 24/7 is beyond far-fetched for the ordinary man, but it doesn't mean sex isn't essential to him. One thing to keep in mind when it comes to bonding with your man via sex is that when in a committed relationship, men correlate sex with love. This is the way they relate to you.

Don't be scared to initiate. Men seek to be desired just as much as women do. You being the one to initiate sex is not only thrilling to him, but also tells him that you want him just as much as he wants you.

2. The Value of Physical Touch

Sex is a vital element of building emotional connection, but so is physical contact. Hold hands, touch his back, embrace, wrap your arms around each other, and kiss him to establish a connection while you're not between the covers.

3. Remain a Mystery

Part of developing an emotional connection is having your man want to devote his time and energy into you. This implies not knowing too much too soon. Many guys find enigmatic women intriguing and many women take advantage of that. You may achieve this by being cautious not to overshare. Sitting down and getting to know every inch of one another's history is a nice sensation, but then you start to realize you know all there is to know. This may lead to boredom. Your life narrative may be the most intriguing he's ever heard, but it can wait until he's utterly infatuated before you reveal it.

4. Take an Interest in his Life

Learn how to connect with your man on an emotional level by showing an interest in his life. Get to know his ideas, desires, and plans for the future. Where does he stand on marriage, his career? Beyond these principles, play a get-to-know-you game. I personally love the 20 question game, it is fun at the same time.

Do so by asking such questions as;

"What was your finest family trip ever and why?"

"Who were you closest to growing up?"

"What occurred to make you laugh the hardest you've ever laughed?"

These questions may be as raunchy or as funny as you desire. From the naughtiest dream he's ever had to would he rather swim in a pool full of Jell-O or a pool full of ice cream, inquiring about these modest minor parts of his life will make him feel important and precious to you. This is a fantastic approach to connect on a deeper level.

5. Take an Interest in his Interests

Men connect emotionally when they have someone to share their hobbies with. This doesn't mean you have to obsess about all of his hobbies and interests, but don't be hesitant to share in them, either. Sit down and watch sports with him. Go on a ride on his motorbike together. Watch his favorite movie. Attend a car exhibition. Make a night of sipping wine and playing multiplayer video games. Most importantly: have fun together.

6. Have an Affirming Attitude

Men like to be around positive women who have an affirming attitude. This doesn't mean you're needed to lavish him with praises all day long merely to maintain his affections, but don't hold back from showing him how much you value him. Too many couples remain silent regarding their mate's great features and this might lead to insecurities. Learn how to connect with your partner on an emotional level by telling him the things you love about him.

7. Show Respect

The more respect you show for your man, the more respect he will have for you. Respect is a type of a strong emotional connection that is a building block for successful partnerships. You may show a guy respect by giving weight to his thoughts, recognizing when is and isn't acceptable to bring up sensitive matters, and providing him room to be himself and to spend time with his friends.

8. Surprise him

Thoughtful presents, experiences, unexpected sex, and spur of the moment evenings out is going to keep your spouse on his toes in the best way imaginable. Just like you, your partner appreciates the comfort of being in a committed relationship, but he needs a little excitement too. Planning trips and offering him surprise presents are a terrific approach to develop an emotional connection by showing him that you care, this one thing I adore doing. Don't buy into the idea that it is a guy's duty to surprise you constantly.

9. Encourage him

To make your partner happy emotionally, you need to know how to encourage him and mean it. You can encourage him by telling him how amazing, talented, or hilarious he is, and to help him pursue his dreams and goals. Don't encourage him if you don't really mean it. You need to be sincere when you help him move forward in life.
If he has a big basketball game coming up, bake him cookies or call him the night before to let him know you care.
If he has a big test, interview, or important event coming up, praise him and let him know how special he is so he feels positive

10. Don't be too Clingy

If you want to make your man happy emotionally, then you have to know how to be there for him when he needs you and how to back off and give him space when he needs it. Being clingy means wanting to hang out with him 24/7, not giving him time to see his boys, and checking in every fifteen seconds when he's not around. Now who likes that? No one, definitely not you.

No matter how serious your relationship is, you shouldn't have to spend every night together. Have a good time going out with your girls and let him go out with his boys without a problem. If you're not hanging out that day, you can check in once or twice, but don't call him every hour, especially when you know he's with his friends, or he'll start to get annoyed.

If you really want to stop being clingy, then you have to be able to pursue your own interests, to have your own passions, and to be your own person without the man's help. You should enjoy your time with your man, but your life shouldn't revolve around him.

11. Learn to Compromise

To make your man happy emotionally, you have to be able to compromise when you have a disagreement. You should know that both of you should be able to get what you want, or to find a middle ground where each of you gets something that makes you happy. Learning to compromise means knowing how to factor in your interests as well as your man's whenever you make a decision.

You can also take turns getting what you want. Maybe you get to pick the restaurant for date night, and he gets to pick the movie. Don't be one of those girls who always gets her way because her man thinks it's easier to give you what you want than to put up a fight.

In a healthy partnership, both individuals should be ready to compromise. Learn to have even-toned talks instead of shouting when you have a dispute.

12. Don't Pick Fight

There's nothing a guy dislikes more than having to battle, feud, or dispute with his lady for no reason. If you have something essential to say, then find a suitable time and location where both of you can concentrate on the topic; don't start ranting at him in public and expect him to interact with you. Learn to keep your voice cool when you disagree instead of increasing it. If you feel the want to start a fight, ask yourself why you want to pick the fight, and what you're actually furious about. Find a method to handle this matter in a mature approach.

13. Remember to have Fun

Some women are so preoccupied with wanting to have a perfect relationship that they forget to relax, kick back, and simply have fun with their partner. Though partnerships are about creating a deep, caring link, they're also about being able to laugh, be funny, and to have a wonderful time without trying too hard. If you and your partner aren't laughing regularly, then he can't be happy emotionally. Don't stress too much about organizing the ideal date or the perfect romantic activity. You may have the greatest fun renting a funny movie, hanging out at the mall, or taking an unplanned vacation to the beach.

14. Keep your Connection Fresh

If you want to keep him satisfied emotionally, then you can't simply settle into the same old pattern, even if you've been together for years. You have to make an effort to keep things new or both of you will lose interest. Here are various methods to accomplish it:
Do something that you've never done before together at least once a month. It may be rock climbing, riding, or playing beach volleyball. Take a dancing lesson together. Learning to salsa or ballroom dance

can help you maintain your body in tune while you explore new vistas.

Find a fresh method to praise your man every week. You can always think of additional things that you adore about him.

Play hard to get once in a while. He shouldn't feel like he can have you anytime he wants. Know that the hunt is never finished. He should be trying as hard to pursue you as he did the day you met.

15. Don't Become Jealous Unreasonably

The quickest way to wreck a fantastic relationship is to start to become overwhelmed with jealousy for no cause at all. If you're jealous, it will simply make your boyfriend upset and frustrated and will make him feel that you're not confident enough in the relationship to believe that he won't cheat on you. If you can't bear it when your guy speaks to or even mentions another female, even if it's absolutely innocent, then you need to focus on keeping your jealousy in control and on making your man feel comfortable.

If you can avoid gossiping or saying negative things about other girls in your orbit, your man will be impressed. Part of being in a good relationship is understanding that there are a lot of other desirable members of the opposite sex out there and accepting that you won't pursue them. If you believe your partner can't be near a gorgeous female without hitting on her, then you have a problem.

16. Don't Attempt to Alter him

If you don't like your guy the way he is to a degree then why bother with him? It's okay to want your man to step it up a bit, whether it's by not showing up late to your dates or by taking less than three hours to return one of your calls, but it's not okay to try to change the way your man looks, dresses, thinks, and talks to suit your idea of what the "perfect man" should be like. This will simply make your guy feel irritated, like he can't be himself, and that you don't like him for who he really is.

If your man is demonstrating less-than-desirable conduct, then it's fair to bring it out. But if you point out every small fault, from the way he eats his food to how he ties his shoes, then he'll feel like you're always nagging him.

Nobody's perfect. You should recognize that there are things about you that your man may not find ideal but that's okay.

17. Make Sure you're Pleased

Though it's crucial for you to make your man happy emotionally and sexually, it's also important that you're feeling emotionally and sexually satisfied in the relationship. It's not the woman's responsibility to tip-toe around the guy, making sure that his wants are addressed. A good partnership is created by shared love, support, and acceptance. If you feel like you spend all of your time thinking about what your man wants instead of being attentive to your own needs, then you have a problem.

Though it's impossible for you and your man to be happy emotionally and sexually 100 percent of the time, you should both be happy the majority of the time for the relationship to thrive.

18. Strategic Space

All relationships require space. Spending time apart is equally as vital as spending time together. Again without his asking, organize a weekend when you two will be able to enjoy yourself without worrying about each other. Take a weekend getaway with pals, drop the kids off at a family member's home and give him the place to himself. Or get him out of the home on a lone expedition to investigate something he's interested in. Giving each other space can help you appreciate each other while you're together.

Men have fundamental requirements that must be addressed to be emotionally content. Your spouse may not overtly ask you to do anything to make him content but it's vital you start someplace and keep it up. He may not even truly realize what needs are and are not being satisfied. So maintain your home happy and start with some fundamental emotionally fulfilling tips.

Chapter 3: Sex and Men

Sex isn't always necessary, but it can be an important part of a healthy, fulfilling relationship. How important it is can vary from one individual to the next. Some people may feel that having a sexual connection with their partner is absolutely vital. Others may feel that other types of intimacy and connection are more important.

In a supportive relationship, there are many benefits to having more sex. Higher rates of sexual activity are linked to positive changes, such as lower blood pressure, reduced stress, greater intimacy, and even a lower divorce rate. While there are no one-size-fits-all rules when it comes to an ideal sex frequency.

How Important is Sex to a Man in a Relationship?

1. It Strengthens the Relationship

Have you heard of sexual afterglow? According to a study, it is a feeling of elevated sexual satisfaction and you can experience it for as long as 48 hours after sex itself. This afterglow helps to enhance the relationship between two couples. In fact, couples who long-term relationships have underlined that a fantastic and passionate sex life plays a key part in their bonding. This is especially true for guys. They regard sex as a method to cement the connection. When their spouse agrees to bedroom action, they are essentially telling them they are a priority.

Men think that sex may assist to feel more bonded even at times when you feel separate. It is not just about physical touch, but also about driving it ahead as a pair.

2. It Helps them Remain Connected to their Spouse

As noted, males consider sex as a method to bond with their mate. Imagine this scenario: You had a quarrel and you haven't talked in many days. Once you began communicating and seeing one other again, guys regard having sex as another method of confirming that your relationship is still solid.

Women incorrectly assume sex to be merely physical. While it might be merely focused on physical requirements occasionally, men in an emotional relationship feel sex is a method for both parties to express love and display a dedication to the couples' connection you created.

3. It Helps them Stay Healthy

Did you know that sexual problems in men may appear due to the lack of sex? There are many health benefits of sex. And it may sound weird, but regular bedroom activity helps to maintain a healthy libido and prevent erectile dysfunction issues, particularly premature ejaculation.

Regular sexual activities also help to avoid low testosterone problems. As men age, their testosterone production reduces and that leads to decreased sex drive and a plethora of other potential issues. Staying active in the bedroom is a way to keep testosterone levels up and remain in shape.

4. It is Far More Effective Than Words

This may be the crucial difference between men and women. Females do not hide the fact that they are more emotional beings than males. They respond to pleasant words and actions and for them showing love via words is a crucial means of creating connection.

While a proverb states that a picture is worth a thousand words, for males in a relationship, sexual intercourse is worth more than a thousand words. That doesn't mean he won't enjoy a kind gesture or good words, but it does imply that there is nothing better a partner can do to communicate love than agree to a passionate night in the bedroom.

5. The Absence of Sex Impacts their Ego

Society wants males to be powerful, but the fact is that they are delicate individuals with an especially sensitive ego. Not only will they will respond when you criticize their looks, but they also perceive a lack of sex as something they should worry about

Believe it or not, sex is one of the things that keep men going. It is a misleading idea that they are selfish, guys want women to enjoy sex too and many are eager to go to great lengths to bring them that happiness.

There is nothing better for a male's ego than when a lady says they liked spending the night with him. Keep in mind that guys may also notice when their spouses are not honest. And while they appreciate compliments, it is vital that they recognize honesty in the one saying them.

If we sum things up, there is only one conclusion we can make: sex is very important for men in a relationship. They see it as one of the staples of partnership and a way to both strengthen the bond and stay close.

That being said, they aren't dedicated to being selfish in bed, contrary to popular belief. Men like praise and enjoying sexual activities, but they are ready to give their best to ensure their partner is having a good time, too. As they see sex as a crucial component of a relationship, men are ready to accept compromises and go the extra mile to ensure that the sex life is functioning perfectly.

Sexual Fantasy

A sexual fantasy or erotic fantasy is a mental picture or pattern of thinking that stirs a person's libido and may cause or increase sexual arousal. A sexual fantasy may be produced by the individual's imagination or memories, and may be activated autonomously or by external stimuli such as erotic literature or pornography, a physical item, or sexual attraction to another person. Anything that may give birth to a sexual arousal may also generate a sexual fantasy, and sexual excitement may in turn give rise to fantasies.

Sexual fantasies are essentially ubiquitous, being recorded in numerous communities around the world. However, because of the nature of certain imaginations, the actual putting of such dreams into reality is significantly less prevalent, owing to cultural, societal, moral, and religious restraints. In some cases, even a discussion by a person of sexual fantasies is subject to social taboos and inhibitions. Some people find it convenient to act out fantasies through sexual roleplay. A person may gain confirmation of a sexual desire by witnessing the representation or discussion of the fantasy in cinema, generally of a pornographic nature. A fantasy may be a positive or negative experience, or even both. It may be in response to a past experience and can influence future sexual behavior.

The Male Sexual Fantasy

Men's sexual fantasies are probably a lot tamer than you think. For the most part, they don't even involve multiple partners, foreign objects or a tight, skimpy French maid's outfit. Male sexual fantasy tends to conform to a fairly strict formula: hot raucous sex with individuals they aren't meant to be doing it with. This pool is enlarged to include platonic friends, our girlfriend or spouse's friends and ex-girlfriends who were fantastic in bed.

Based on the men I've talked to about this, I'd have to say they're not all the same. Some allegedly popular male sexual fantasies (two women at once, for example) that I know appeal to some guys I've met, don't even make sense to my husband. I've found myself attempting to explain things to him as he stares at me with a 'this is simply odd' attitude! And I've met some males who truly dreamt about violent sex or BDSM that would freak out others.

Here are some answers from certain individuals;

Anonymous 1: Almost every male I know wants a threesome, involving two ladies. However, if I teasingly say that I want a threesome (I have no real interest in one) with my man and another man, they in no way want a part of it! Double standard! A couple more that man friends have shared with me are ladies who are completely shaved and being recorded having sex.

Anonymous 2: I personally know my boyfriend's dream is to be with another guy. He wants simply oral contact and to feel the sensation of another man's touch. I aid him with this via internet/video/porn or simply rating men in the mall. It makes him more at ease and very, very into me. I do not feel intimidated or jealous, as we both recognize it is fiction and he has no actual desire to experience it in the flesh. But I absolutely back him and appreciate the fact he shared me his deepest, darkest, sex desire.

Anonymous 3: I just discovered out my husband's desire was to have anal sex after uncovering his online searches. At first, I was repulsed, then we tried it and it hurt at first but now I truly like it. We are waiting now to complete my wish to witness him with another lady. Yeah most males fantasize about that I know and mine is no different, but he never addressed it as he believed it was too off limits. Should have seen his mouth drop. Anyway, we are in the process of making that happen. I have no clue why I, as the woman, want to witness this but it demonstrates that it is not only a man's thing.

What am merely trying to say is that you should try as much as possible to fit into your guy sexual fantasy, it absolutely going to have him hooked up on you.

How to Make your Guy Sexually Active

It's not always simple to make your partner satisfied emotionally and sexually in a relationship. To make your man happy emotionally, you have to be sensitive to his needs and to know when to give him space. To make your man happy sexually, you have to desire to do new things and to be daring and adventurous. But the most crucial thing is that you are feeling delighted when you're with him.

While there is no Holy Grail for enhancing sexual stamina for every guy, there are several basic things to help men perform better and longer. Sexual stamina and, more crucially, developing sexual stamina is something most men think about often which in turn influences their sexual activities with their lady. As a woman you may aid gently in keeping your guy not only emotionally content, but also sexually fulfilled.

For most males, concern about staying power is right up there with their anxiousness over penis size when it comes to measuring their sexual aptitude. Luckily, there is a little bit of good news. The following recommendations assist your guy get started on your road to supercharging his sexual stamina. Ready to get started?

Tips To Boost Sexual Stamina in Your Man

1. Stay Active

Staying Active Helps Boost Stamina. Exercising helps you accomplish more than simply look amazing. It is a terrific approach to enhance sexual stamina. After all, sex is simply a sort of exercise, and it can really get the heart pounding if you do it correctly. While a romp in the sack isn't like running the Boston Marathon, 20 to 30 minutes of exercise two to three times a week can maintain your heart healthy enough for sex.

Doctors normally suggest that you can walk up two flights of stairs without breathing significantly before getting too frisky and I surely do agree with that.

2. Eat Your Fruits And Vegetables.

Foods That Boost Stamina in Bed. Your mama knows best. Fruits and veggies truly do help your guy grow large and powerful. A good diet is one of the greatest methods to boost sexual stamina naturally. Apples, broccoli, and peppers carry the antioxidant quercetin recognized for aiding to boost endurance. Don't forget an additional slice or two of watermelon, an L-arginine-rich meal. Wash it all down with pomegranate juice, which is wonderful for improving blood flow.

3. Get A Little Help with a Delay Spray

Promescent climax control delay spray is scientifically proven to help last longer in bed. For women who seek a more reliable approach to enhance their spouse sexual stamina, having a little more aid from science is no shame. Delay sprays can help prolong the time it takes to reach an orgasm with a high satisfactory rate. There are dozens of brands you can pick from, but they are not all the same. For the greatest experience, search for a product that is entirely absorbed by your skin.

4. Omega-3 Fatty Acids

Omega-3 fatty acids are believed to stimulate mental sharpness, improve sleep quality, and strengthen the immune system. Still, it is also a terrific strategy to maintain your heart health and lessen joint discomfort. A strong heart and flexibility are two things you can't get enough of in the sack.
The better a guy feels, the longer they can go. Fatty fish like tuna and salmon are rich providers of Omega-3 fatty acids, as well as avocados and olive oil.

5. Reduce Your Stress, Boost Your Sex

Stress elevates blood pressure, and that's a killer in and out of the bedroom. Quote: Stress not only damages male sexual stamina, but it is a frequent cause for erectile dysfunction and premature ejaculation.

You may assist in regulating stress in your spouse's life by taking up meditation or yoga. If he suffers from disorders such as ED or PE that leads him to feel shame, talking to your spouse outside of romantic times might help soothe the mind.

6. Stop Smoking Cigarette

There are tons of reasons to stop smoking, but if you need another one, giving up your tobacco habit may boost your sexual stamina. Research shows that smoking can have a number of negative impacts on a guy's sexual health including: lowering libido, decreasing physical endurance, reducing the quality of your erections. In fact, smoking is directly correlated with increased chances of erectile dysfunction.

Unfortunately, switching to vaping won't help either. Studies reveal that no matter the administration mechanism, nicotine may diminish sexual desire.

7. Stop or Reduce Drinking Alcohol

Alcohol Decreases Sexual Performance. Every guy knows that drinking too much can lead to disappointment in the lovemaking department. Helping your man in quitting or reducing alcohol intake can help build up your sexual stamina in the bedroom by reducing the chances of weight gain, reduce circulation, poor heart health, depression, lower libido

8. Pick the Proper Position

Sex standing up can improve sexual stamina in men. We all have our own unique anatomical quirks that make us favor one sexual position over another. If you are looking to get better endurance in the bedroom, you and your partner should try choosing a position less stimulating.

Many guys find they can last longer when they have sex if their partner is on top. The penis will get less stimulation in these types of positions and help get better stamina. Having sex in the standing position also tends to prolong the time before having an orgasm.

9. Switch up Your Technique

Besides changing sexual positions, you may want to think about talking to your partner about new thrusting patterns which helps him last longer in bed. Most guys like to go as hard and as fast as possible. Doing this not only makes them climax quicker, but they also tire themselves out, leaving their partners unfulfilled.

He should try experimenting by adjusting the depth of his thrusts from shallow to deep, as well as the speed of the thrusts. Most guys tend to last longer when they use more shallow thrusts since the head of the penis is less stimulated, but play around and see what works for you both.

10. Improve Your Sleep, Improve Your Sex Stamina

Do you stay out late partying on the weekends? If you want to have more and better sex, don't. Research reveals that gaining an additional hour or two of sleep might aid enhanced stamina and of course, much more energy to endure. Remember that most individuals have a greater quality of sleep after sex, so it is a self-feeding loop of wonderful sleep and amazing sex.

11. Get him coffee From the Local Coffee Shop before Getting It On

Research from the University of Texas indicated that males who drank one or two cups of coffee each day were not as likely to exhibit symptoms of ED as those who refrained from coffee. Don't worry if he can't tolerate coffee, caffeine appears to be the most crucial ingredient? Two cups of coffee provide roughly 180 mg of caffeine, but so does 90 grams of dark chocolate.

12. Use a Thicker Condom

Too much sensitivity can lower men sexual stamina. Many guys find a simple solution is wearing a condom or switching to a thicker condom if already using one. Brands don't usually advertise their condoms as thicker, so you will want to look for words on the packaging like "Extra Strength" or "Extra Safe." Besides helping to boost sexual stamina, condoms are a must for preventing STDs.

13. Why Not Give Edging A Try?

Edging goes by a variety of various names, such as the stop and start approach and the squeeze technique. The key aim is for a guy to get himself to the point just before he ejaculates and then to restore control by minimizing stimulation. Mastering the edging process does require time and effort, and it is not always the most practical choice, but there are numerous advantages. Edging specialists typically say that not only can they control their ejaculations, but also experience greater, more powerful orgasms. Some even claim to have numerous orgasms.

14. Get in Some Kegel Exercises

All the way around, Kegel (pelvic floor) exercises are healthy for your guy, even if the prevailing belief is these exercises solely assist the female population. As a guy, strengthening the pelvic floor may provide better control over ejaculations, which is a clear bonus if striving for a longer experience.

In one research, 82.5 percent of males who conducted pelvic floor exercises saw an increase in sexual stamina, rather outstanding results for sure. Basically, Kegels entail identifying the muscles utilized to control the flow when one pee. Once detected, he may tense these muscles and also repeat sets to increase strength and muscular tone.

15. Stay Hydrated

Staying hydrated is vital for greater men's stamina. Hydration is highly crucial to a guy stamina with any physical activity, including sex. For one, he's less likely to feel dehydrated midway through a lengthy session and get in a rush. But, most significantly, taking in adequate H2O promotes greater blood flow to the penis. With adequate water, blood volume rises, which helps blood flow through arteries and veins without as much effort.

Another crucial point to notice, when dehydrated, is that a male body may create angiotensin, which causes constriction of the blood vessels. This reduced blood flow might make it tougher to retain an erection. Ideally, males should take in 3.7 liters of fluid on a daily basis, potentially more if they have greater activity levels.

16. Steer Clear Of Simple Carbs

Before sex, make sure he's receiving a nice balance of complex carbs. On the contrary, complex carbohydrates break down slowly, which gives more steady energy levels. You can discover complex carbohydrates in foods like: Oatmeal, quinoa, or whole wheat bread, Sweet potatoes, dried beans and legumes, Brown or wild rice.

Simple carbohydrates may deliver a burst of energy, but the increase is short-lived. You obtain more simple carbohydrates from meals with high sugar content, such as fruits and milk.

17. Practice the Stop-Squeeze Method

The stop-squeeze approach, often dubbed the squeeze technique, is a simple strategy to pause your roll during sex, and it may really lead to greater ejaculation control. Essentially, stop-squeeze includes pulling out when you feel ejaculation approaching near and squeezing the head or frenulum of the penis hard for around five seconds or until the impulse to ejaculate diminishes.

After a little delay, when out of the red zone, you may continue. Getting part in this process as a girl may be a lot of fun.

18. Get Some Sun

Sunshine is not only excellent for the spirit, but also beneficial for the male body when it comes to sexual performance. So, if you're searching for a free boost for your man, getting some sun may do him some good.

If he spends a lot of time inside, as many people do, attempt to aid in making an effort to go out in the sunshine for 30 minutes or so when feasible. Sun exposure raises vitamin D levels, and vitamin D has been related with greater erectile performance and higher libido.

In one research, males who were given vitamin D supplements showed enhanced sexual performance and even an increase in natural, free testosterone levels.

19. Take a Time Out for Foreplay

Simply said, if you're having an issue bridging the gap between you and your lover, consider slowing things down a little. Instead of a guy going all-in till ejaculation with straight-up intercourse, take pauses here and there for foreplay. Engaging in a little pleasure might give him time to calm down. While taking a time-out may seem like edging and may have comparable features, time-outs are not completely the same. You may just opt to take a break any moment throughout penetration, even if you're not near to ejaculation at all.

20. Try a New Environment

Consistency is not always key when it comes to sex. Sometimes, breaking the humdrum of the same old routine can breathe new life into a sexual encounter, regardless of what sexual woes you may be facing. For example, if you and your partner are normally bedroom-business, missionary-style participants, the same environment and usual methodology can leave you in the same old mindset. This can be problematic if your man has issues with performance anxiety, erectile dysfunction, and even stamina.

The sameness of the occasion can encourage those usual thoughts and feelings that get in the way. Consider making out-of-the-ordinary sex a goal. Maybe you could rent a hotel room for the night, initiate sex in another room of the house, or even simply give the bedroom a slight makeover with different lighting, music, or arrangements. Slight modifications might frequently be enough to send you into an entirely new mental frame for sex.

Chapter 4: Make him Ache For You

Okay, I don't know who needs to hear this, but let me just start by saying you are a goddamn treasure. If you're with a guy who doesn't make you feel loved or worthy every single minute, oh girl, make him ache for you.

Or you becoming out of touch with your man particularly in your sex life, which is already creating fractures and rough edges. But he's a nice guy you love so much and don't want to lose him. Here are a few pointers to get him hooked on you.

But if he does make you feel loved and valued consistently, you just simply want to do something a little more for him from time to time, I fully understand it. And boy, oh boy, do we have some seductive suggestions for you.

The good news: These strategies work regardless of your dating situation. I don't care whether you've been together five years or you're on your first month of dating. Trust me there's something in here for your guy that will truly make him ache for you and maybe even beg, if you're into that sort of thing.

1. Show off Your Curves and Create Some Eye Contact

Yup, sometimes all it takes is a brief little tease of your body's contours to make a man's mouth drop. By playing up your "S" stance as much as possible. "Hips out, head slanted, shoulders asymmetrical, and curves anywhere else you can manage."

Another good tip: Give him a taste of the eye triangle. Make direct eye contact, then shift your gaze down their shoulders, down their torso, and then rapidly back up.

2. Be Independent

When I say independent, I mean eat what you want, listen to your favorite music, go out with your ladies for frequent brunch dates, and continue to indulge in all of your favorite activities.
An independent woman is more desirable to a guy because he is challenged that she can survive without him, make him feel that you enjoy hanging out with him, but you still have a life of your own to live at the same time.

3. Tease him While you're Messaging

A bit of an apparent one, but not usually used. Sexting is an incredible game changer and it doesn't have to be hard. You might start by indicating that you're desiring him. Say something like, "Wow, your touch would feel so amazing right now." And if you want to really improve your chances of having him ache for you, "send him a photo of you lying down with your rear arched up," and watch how he salivates.

4. Utter the One Word That Drives Him Nuts

As lovey-dovey as pet names make him feel, they still don't compare to the explosive sensation your guy receives when his name crosses your lips. Just hearing that is an aphrodisiac, it ratchets up his desire because the message you give is 'It's you I'm thinking about and no one else.' And males need to hear that it's related to their fundamental need to win out all the competitors."
For instance, when you're feeling sexy in a public situation, like in a dark bar, insert it into conversation in unexpected areas and stop for a second or two: "And then...Jeremy...I pulled my clothes behind me."
Or try another tactic while he's making the moves on you: Just sort of coo his name to bring his concentration totally on to you. "When

Jake and I are getting it on, sometimes it seems like he's lost in his own brain," says Marilynn, 26. "But when I scream his name, everything seems like it grows hotter between us, like it drags him into the experience."

5. Reach inside His Pocket for the Keys

Well, more than just the keys. The lesson is this: never underestimate the power of an unexpected touch, just by activating his nerve endings when he's not prepared for it, you establish a pleasant physical connection that leaves your guy wanting more. Even better, your man unconsciously becomes hooked on those mini-moments of excitement and desires them when you're not there. From now on, stay on the lookout for good occasions to touch him "accidentally." For example, don't ask him for his keys...glide your hand into his pocket and gently pull them out. Don't ask him to pass the salt...reach across him, letting your breasts touch against his arm. Don't go by him in a packed bar...press your buttocks against his gear. According to Alicia, 35, these stealth strikes work like a charm. "If I've been particularly touchy-feely with Jake, the following morning, he'll be incredibly cozy," she explains. "It's like he wants to be closer to me."

6. Make Small Changes for Big Results

Men register eye-catching changes to your appearance, and it draws them to you, adding novelty will keep his desire for you strong.
There's a catch though, if you want to snag his immediate interest, the change has to be guy-visible. To activate his desire, it has to be a departure from your everyday look, maybe take a break from your jeans routine and strut around in a miniskirt. Wear a noticeably higher heel. Or ditch your bra for a day and put a little extra bounce in your step.

7. Compliment Him the Right Way

Look, men love flattery. More than anything, men desire the feeling of being desired. When a man hears praise from his partner, it reinforces that she's attracted to him, which further intensifies his feelings for her.

But there's a trick to buttering up your guy right. You see, men are super sensitive to gushing. It makes them want to gag and run far away. So when you give him props, stick to this tip: The more obscure and exclusive the praise to him, the more genuine it feels. That's why Polly, 40 casually praises her guy's kitchen-cleaning prowess. "Tom is anal about wiping down the counters, so whenever I go to cook and they're clean, I say how much I love it." He may dismiss your flattery with a grunt, but deep down, he's loving every second of it.

8. Give Him a Sensory Flashback

Think about when you first fell for your guy. What reminds you both of that time (aside from the conniption fit you had every time the phone rang)? Figure it out and you've found the secret to conjuring up that new-love rush. When he experiences something that he associates with falling in love with you, those intense, sensual memories trigger a positive physical reaction and generate instant longing.

The smell of sunscreen and chlorine makes me crave my wife," says Peter, 58. "It takes me back to when we were in high school and she worked summers as a lifeguard at a pool. Smelling that scent gives me the jolt all over again." To get your guy in the moment, revive an old brand of perfume, visit a favorite place from your shared past, or reinstate an early dating ritual. Oftentimes, you won't even need to say anything. These sensory connections are so strong that he'll be transported back instantly.

9. Keep Things Mysterious, at Least a Little Bit

Your man is an explorer by nature. The less he knows, the more he wants to know. That's why you stimulate his interest when you don't first divulge your deepest ideas. Obviously tell him when you had a horrible day and need to speak things out, but don't be scared to be a bit subtle from time to time.

10. Take Use of Your Seductive Smell

Biologists say the reason your odor turns him on is because scent is one of the most primal senses, it goes a direct path to the brain's limbic lobe, where it may trigger an emotional response. Spray your preferred scent on his pillow before you leave. He'll never want to get out of bed.

You are a Seductress

When it comes to enticing a guy, only appearances aren't enough. Sure that could attract any guy's attention, but there's a lot more than that when it comes to being sexy. Appealing lips mean nothing if a lady doesn't know how to pick the correct phrases that would stimulate a man's attention. The art of seduction is a lot more than 'dress to impress and am here to tell you everything about becoming a seductress.

What Precisely is a Seductress?

The term "seductress" has a negative rep. When we hear the term seductress we automatically get a picture of a temptress that leaves men drooling as she comes across the room. Or with their eyes bulging out of their heads. While some women may prefer this sort of attention, not all women who want to feel sexy want to be regarded in this manner.

Now, another thing I've heard previously is that a seductress is practically the same thing as a home-wrecker, but I think this to be pretty absurd. You don't have to take another woman's man if you want to be considered sexy.

The last preconceived notion I'd like to debunk about what it means to be seductive is that you have to be impossibly beautiful. Seductiveness isn't synonymous with physical beauty. The most important element of seductiveness is loving yourself and being confident about what you bring to the table.

So, what is a seductress? In my opinion, a seductress is a woman who presents an exciting challenge, a woman who can be in control of any situation, and a woman who is confident about herself. She doesn't try to be like others; she knows that she is special and she's not going to beg for anyone's attention. She isn't easily attainable and her confidence makes her magnetic and attractive. She doesn't flirt with just everyone; only a man of interest to her. She's naturally sexy and knows how to highlight her most attractive qualities.

So I think you can see where I'm going here. What is the key ingredient? Confidence!!!

To seduce a man, you first need to seduce yourself. Learn to be yourself. Forget about all the expensive things that will make you look instantly pretty. Forget about the imposed beauty standards and focus only on yourself. What are the things you like the most about yourself? Are you curious, extroverted, caring, and generous? What are the things that you'd like to change about yourself? Seducing yourself is about being in touch with your true self. To seduce a man, you need to know who you are and what you offer. Self-confidence is something you can't buy. It comes from within you and not from other trivial things. Fall in love with your imperfections and you'll boost your confidence. Show the world that you're proud of who you are and you will seduce any man you desire.

The first thing a man notices about you is your vibe. Women usually don't pay that much attention to how they feel about themselves because they're only focusing on how others perceive them. Everything about your personality makes you who you are. The first thing a man notices about you is not what you're wearing but your vibe. If you're wearing what makes you feel comfortable, it will show in your attitude. If you're not, you'd rather look frustrated or annoyed. How do you then seduce anyone if you're not feeling good about yourself in the first place? One genuine smile has the power to seduce any man out there. It will show him you don't take yourself too seriously and that you're in a good mood and fun to be around. When you pass a smile to a man, make sure you make eye contact for a few seconds. This will hold his attention.

You need to learn how to flirt with your words and body language. Pay more attention to what you're going to say instead of what you're going to wear. It sure is impossible to predict the flow of the conversation, but it's very important to say the right words at the right time. Don't say the first thing that comes to your mind, create a mystery and build it up in a flirty way. If a man asks you a question and you give the answer immediately, there's no seduction. But if you keep him guessing, he will be simmering for some time until you finally give him the answer. Seduction is about maintaining mystery, playing with words, being creative and giving him everything bit by bit. It's also about giving out hits with your body language. It's a powerful tool to use with the right words. A subtle tough, locking eyes, playing with your hair, being spontaneous - all of it will seduce him. Avoid crossing your arms because that's a huge sign of a reserved person. You can seduce a man with your intelligence, sense of humor, spontaneity, body language, all of it without taking your clothes off or touching him. Men sure are visual creatures, but the physical appearance will only catch their attention. It's your personality that will capture their heart and seduce their mind.

5 Types of Seductress

Women learned early on that one of the ways to gain power in a patriarchal society was to become a seductress. Cleopatra, Xi Shi and Empress Justinia are a few that come to mind from history. In the midcentury we had Marilyn Monroe, Bettie Page and Heddy Lamar, to name a few.

In seduction, the woman is no longer a passive sex object, she has become an active agent, a figure of power. The trick is to lure a man in through cleverness and creativity. Then turn the dynamic around to create true power.

1. The Siren

Aphrodite, the goddess of love and sex, embodies this seductress archetype. The siren is the male fantasy of sexual and confident female. She offers endless pleasure and a hint of danger.

Cleopatra was a spectacular siren. To protect Egypt, she put Julius Caesar and Mark Antony under her spell. She offered constant variety and with a promise of adventure. Marilyn Monroe was a sex siren. Her innocence and vulnerability, combined with her sexuality, proved irresistible.

A highly feminine and sexual presence will quickly differentiate you, since most women lack the confidence to project such an image.

2. The Ideal Lover

The Ideal Lover studies her conquest, goes along with his moods and finds out what is missing from his life. This seductress appeals to people's idealized visions of themselves. She makes them feel elevated, noble, spiritual, and this magic keeps them seduced.

The Ideal Lover wins through her self-sacrifice, devotion and patient attention. This is a rare seductress because it takes effort. This is the type of seductress you find when young women seduce wealthy older men.

3. The Natural

Naturals keep their childish enthusiasm and energy. They appear to be open and not beaten down by the world. They are playful, brazen and have a lighthearted spirit. The Natural works best when the seductress is young. An older Natural needs to temper her playfulness with adult experience and wisdom.

People are drawn to those who expect a lot out of life…Wild independence has a provocative effect on us.

4. The Coquette

Coquettes play a delicate game of push and pull with their targets. Powerful men love a challenge. The Coquette pulls men in with sexual appeal and charm, and then leaves them unsatisfied. She forces them to chase after her.

Self-confident and independent, the Coquette never gives off a needy or desperate vibe. She will not do things out of duty and is never jealous.

They bait with the promise of reward, the hope of physical pleasure, happiness, fame, power all of which proves elusive, yet this only makes their targets pursue them more.

5. The Charmer

The Charmer creates a relaxed atmosphere and listens. She observes the target to determine their needs. Charmers never talk about themselves. Rather, they appear interested and focused on the other person.

How to be a Seductress Starting Today

Before we go into the specifics, I wanted to go over some general tips for being a seductress. One of the more important things to keep in mind when you want to seduce someone is body language.

Just think about it, you can be the most strikingly beautiful woman in the entire universe, but if your body language makes you seem like you aren't confident or like you are quite uncomfortable, you are going to give your target a very different image of yourself. Now, if you know how to adopt proper body language, your odds of making him fall for you are going to skyrocket. Sure, some men like shy, timid women, but a seductress is confident and magnetic for this very reason.

Look him directly in the eye when you're speaking to one another. Square your shoulders to face him and don't hesitate to smile. It's ideal to be inviting and to make him want to spend more time with you. I see a lot of people making the mistake of thinking that a seductress has to be cold and maybe even borderline mean, but that doesn't need to be the case.

So think about being tactile as well. For example, touch his arm when he makes you laugh. Think about the way he's seeing you and think about the image you're portraying.

Let's take a look at some of the things you can start doing today so that you can start feeling and being more seductive.

1. Maintain a Bit of Mystery and this goes for Both Clothing and Actions

You don't have to be scantily clad to seduce a man, and you don't need to tell him about your intentions. In fact, it's best if he's not sure whether or not you're into him. The more he gets to mull it over and begin to wonder if you're interested, the more likely it is that his interest will peak as well! So let him wonder and hope and make him want to work for it. Don't flat out tell him that you want him, and don't chase after him.

2. Always Remember to Have Fun

I often see people start to put unnecessary pressure on themselves and on the relationship by focusing too much on the future, where things are going, and they begin to obsess over little things. Adopting a reasonable, carefree attitude further illustrates how good you feel in your skin, with or without your man.

3. Make your Conversations and the Time you Spend Together Interesting

It's fairly basic, the more a guy likes spending time with you, the more likely he will be to constantly return back for more. Playing too hard to get might result in your target just losing interest.

Seducing a guy isn't simply physical. In truth, the physical part is quite negligible. Stimulating a guy cognitively is the approach to develop his attraction to you. Of course, physical attraction is crucial and thrilling, but more is required if you want to build a relationship that lasts for a long time. So, make sure you're interested, that you're learning, that you're open to new experiences, and don't be scared to share this experience and information with this guy. Fascinating individuals attract others!

4. Make Sure that you Always Have your Own Thing going on

So many individuals lose focus of their own goals and projects when they begin dating someone or are married, don't fall into this trap since maintaining personal life and accomplishing the things that are important to you are some of the sexiest attributes a person can have. One of the finest methods to be sexy is by retaining your independence and showing him that you don't need him all the time. When someone is too easily accessible all the time no matter what the surprise and the challenge are no longer present.

5. If you Work with him, Show him that You Work Hard and are Enthusiastic About your Assignments But you Also Know How to Have Fun

A determined woman is highly appealing, and if you combine that with your confident attitude, then you can guarantee that guys will be stealing glimpses at you left and right throughout the workplace. If on top of that you let your hair down at the end of the day today, and self-assuredly stroll out of there, odds are you'll ignite some dreams.

How to be Beautiful and Alluring by Being Independent

While we're talking about how to seduce someone and how to be seductive, we tend to concentrate on what to do when you're together. Truth be told, you can make a man desire you even when you're not physically in the same spot. The idea is to demonstrate to him that you don't genuinely need him.

I know that may seem weird when you first read it, but think about it. You're a strong, active lady who is enjoying her life, visiting her friends, working on her tasks. You're not constantly phoning him and you don't always have time to visit him. When you do see him, he feels delighted that he's finally had you all to himself, so it's instantly simpler for you to seduce him.

You can really utilize social media as a terrific tool for this. Post images on Facebook or Instagram of the fun and exciting activities you've been doing either on your own or with friends, and he will want to be a part of it.

If you've already begun dating or married, instead of concentrating on the relationship and on simply constantly being together, change your attention to sharing memorable moments together, and to experience new things. Freshness is one of the most attractive aspects a relationship may have. This is incredibly crucial since a lot of women tend to obsess on the relationship (and not on how to captivate a man and keep things new,) and in turn end up letting it get a little stale! Always make sure you do what's in your power to maintain the connection secure from boredom or too much predictability.

If you really want to get creative with seduction, use the 5 senses.

1. The Sense of Sight

Men are visual animals and this may be exploited to your advantage. Let him feast his eyes over you. But as I mentioned before, not all of you. Less is absolutely more, particularly in the early years of dating or wooing someone.

It has been demonstrated that both men and women appear to link the color red with passion and desire. No one is fully sure why, Perhaps because it makes us think of red roses or Valentine's Day. Whatever the cause may be, utilize it to your advantage! Another one of the finest methods to entice a guy is grabbing his attention with what's on your body. On your next date, wear a red dress or a red blouse. Red lipstick looks wonderful too, but use your discretion since some men could be less prone to kissing red as they don't want to wind up wearing the lipstick as well.

2. The Sense of Smell

You, of course, want to smell nice and have a fresh breath, but the sense of smell extends much deeper than simply cleanliness. If you're seeking hot ideas on how to captivate a guy, start thinking about making him hooked to your smell. Everyone has their own distinct aroma, and if you get near enough to smell it, you may pick up on it and be hooked. Though we don't frequently think about this since it's a subconscious, primitive inclination, it doesn't mean we can't play with it.

You may be wondering how you can make him fall for you by utilizing the sense of smell, well, here's an example; if you're saying goodbye at the end of an evening, embrace him and let the hold linger for a little. Give him a minute to genuinely get extremely near to you and unconsciously pick up on the closeness of being so close to your flesh.

Another thing you may do is to spritz a tiny quantity of your favorite perfume into your hair and put it up in a ponytail. When you're next to him, let your hair down and he'll receive an unexpected whiff of your unique perfume and he'll immediately feel closer to you and more intimate. You've heard that scent is the strongest sense related to memory right?

3. Sound

This is an extremely handy tool if you're already started to date the person you've had your eye on or married. Many women don't speak about what turns them on to their partner but if the occasion presents itself, why not whisper something wicked in his ear?

You can do it while you're alone, but you might also do it in public. While you're among friends, whisper what you plan to do to him later, and then continue continuing your chat with the others. He will be wondering whether he heard it accurately and his attention will be awakened. I bet he'll have difficulties focusing on the remainder of the chat with the group after that.

4. The Perception of Taste

This is also a little simpler if you're already getting intimate with this guy. You may use a blindfold and don't even have to be in the bedroom. It might be at the dinner table and you can start to feed him and play with your food.

When one of these five senses is taken away, the other ones are heightened. If you're offering him a cherry, let it touch his lips. Then, when he least expects it, instead of fetching something to eat, let him feel your lips on his. The element of surprise, the blindfold, and the fact that you're so in charge will undoubtedly turn him on.

5. The Sensation of Touch

The sense of touch goes hand in hand with the part of body language that I was talking over earlier. That said, be cautious not to overdo it. Avoid touching him excessively since it might become strange.

Instead, catch him off surprise with your leg brushing his beneath the table.

If it's the first phase of your venture, you'll want to go for more delicate seduction strategies such as talk, mild touches, and body language. In discussion you want him to start to question whether you're actually interested in him, and make him want to continue revealing facts about himself with you. If he's telling you about one of his interests, ask him crucial questions and let him know that you're paying attention.

Very important; don't stop being a seductress after you're in a relationship with him. Many individuals make the mistake of being extremely seductive up until they achieve a connection with their goal. They don't do it on purpose, they simply unconsciously think that they don't need to attempt to entice him anymore since they're already together.

The fact is that the death of desire leads to the demise of many relationships, thus retaining seduction is truly the key to maintaining an interesting relationship that never becomes monotonous. The trick to keep attraction alive in a relationship is simply to be imaginative. Invite your spouse to do activities you've never done before, or to see locations you've never seen before. You can continue seducing your man by surprising him with some new lingerie or keys to a hotel room for the night.

Passion and excitement are crucial at any stage of the relationship, even if you've been together for twenty years. Human people need to be stimulated, and this is one of the secrets to making your relationship endure the test of time.

So few people ever listen, that this attention builds a powerful spell. The Charmer appeals to the suppressed or rejected elements of individuals and makes them feel like the star. This in turn, makes them adore the Charmer.

Abolish Anti-seductive Qualities in Yourself

Many individuals have a preconceived sense of what it means to be a seductress and they end up behaving in ways that they expect a seductress to behave, but the effect is simply that the guy they seek loses interest.

First of all, and as I stated before, it's crucial that you should not expose your intentions, he shouldn't know that you're actively attempting to seduce him. This would make it too simple for him to assume that he's got you under his thumb and then the mystery and thrill disappear into thin air.

Here is something that is very important. I was working with a geologist who had problems attracting the man she was interested in because of the manner she was dealing with him. She had been thinking that by appearing confident, she also needed to emasculate the man. Don't throw the person down or laugh at him if he's being honest. Sure, you want to be hard to get, but not to the point that he would no longer want to even attempt. Men often don't enjoy being treated like a boy or being talked to in a condescending way.

Another thing to pay attention to is making sure that you're not being needy or clinging. Begging for his attention is not going to raise his enthusiasm. If you want to be a seductress, you want to offer him the opportunity to hope you call him, to hope he gets a chance to see you. He should realize that you've got your own stuff going on, and he's not the only thing on your mind.

Just as important as the ability to seduce is to not have any anti-seductive qualities. The key trait that repels people is insecurity. Evidence of this feature includes a lack of giving, not only of money, but also of time and attention.

Other anti-seductive behaviors include forceful argumentation or behaving judgmental. Windbags and folks who speak too much demonstrate their narcissism. False attempts at attention, like effusive praise or stifling affection repel. They expose deep gaps of need that make the victim go in the opposite way.

Anti-Seducers are the opposite: insecure, self-absorbed and unable to fathom the psychology of another person, they actually repel.

How to Evolve From Plain Jane to Sweet Seductress

Desire starts in the brain. So start with that instrument in the north before going to his organ in the south. Got a hot date booked for this evening? One that you sense is going to lead to the bedroom? With your spouse or absolute stranger? Begin your dance of seduction during the day. Send him hot texts throughout the afternoon: "I can't wait to see you tonight", "I'm thinking about your gorgeous mouth", "I'm imagining what it will be like when you undress me." See what you are doing there? Each text gets a little more daring, a little hotter. By the time you meet your date at the restaurant, he's going to have to hold himself back from tearing your clothes off of you. Make him wait until after dessert and coffee.

Clothing

The common thought is that certain ways of dressing are guaranteed to arouse a man. Typically this would be a low-cut dress, high heels, and fishnet stockings. Iconic lingerie would include a lacy bra, garter belt and black stockings. Yes, most men find all this to be sexy, but the best way to turn on your man would be to find out what he likes, specifically. You don't have to ask him directly, you might point out certain celebrities and ask if he likes their style. You'll quickly learn if your guy is more into sexy athletic wear (like a sweatshirt unzipped just enough to sneak a peek!) or if he is more of a classic guy who appreciates the tight red slit gown.

Of course, it's always easier to just pose the question straight out, in your fantasies, how do you like your partner to dress? If you want to get right to the point. The idea of almost being able to see your underwear (if you are wearing any) but not quite? It will drive your guy crazy with lust.

Touch

Men are thought to be very penis-centered in terms of what turns them on. But in fact, there are endless ways to seduce your man before you get to his favorite plaything. In fact, by deliberately not starting with his penis you will enhance his sexual pleasure just by anticipation, where is she going to stroke me next? Will be one hottest thought in his head as you make love.

If you really want to give your partner pure pleasure, start with his mouth, with a long session of intimate kissing. While you are concentrating on his lips and his tongue, remove his shirt and caress his torso, his shoulders, and his neck. Yes, he will be dying for you to move your hands southward, but linger elsewhere. Slowly release his belt, remove his trousers and boxer shorts. Explore his waist, his thigh everywhere but where he wants you to go. Then, when both of you cannot stand it anymore, proceed to the center of his world. Watch his reaction and congratulate yourself on your patience and tactile skills!

Massage

Want to combine both relaxation and sexual tension? Massage your man. Grab some professional-grade massage oil and start with his shoulders and back. After that, have him turn over and do his chest. For a truly erotic experience, don't get to the happy ending too soon. Have him hold off so you can offer him the most blissful, muscle-relaxing massage he'll ever have.

Get on up

Sure, the classic missionary position is a tried-and-true way for both of you to give and receive pleasure. But never underestimate the seductive power when you get on top of him. The view from his perspective your face, your breasts, your body in motion is hugely erotic for him.

Take control. Be the director in bed

Even the most successful alpha-male enjoys handing over the sexual reins every now and then. So slip into your most domineering persona and have it your way. Be the director in bed, you decide how much foreplay is enough, what position to start with, when to transition to another, who is the recipient of oral sex first, and of course who gets the first climax. You'd be surprised at how many powerful men find being submissive to be very hot.

Talk Dirty to him

Even before seeing it on internet porn, men loved the idea of their partner having a dirty mouth. Especially if you are Miss Prim by day, the contrast is very erotic to them. So surprise your guy by whispering very explicitly what you'd like him to do to you while you are having sex. Tell him what you'd like to do to him. And make your orgasm very, very known. He won't be able to control himself.

Self-pleasure

Your man would love to watch you turn yourself on but may have been too timid to ask you to do this. So turn it into a show just for him. The only rule? He can't join in the fun until you tell (or beg) him to. Have him sit back and watch you for as long as you'd like him to.

Chapter 5: His Secret Sex Zones

Ladies, if you want to give your man the best bedroom experience of his life, trust me, it's really not at all difficult to do it. You just need to know how to touch a man (your man obviously) . Pleasing your man in bed is not rocket science if you know what his hot-spots are. So, instead of limiting yourself to just his package, it's time for you to explore the rest of his body too.
Let's talk about arousal. You probably already know there are tons of different ways to set the vibes before sex. Your sex playlist, where

you go at it, and how you go about touching your partner all play a major role in your overall sexperience. But what turns one person on might not do the job for another, which is where things can get complicated. The good news is, even though everyone's different, when hooking up with a guy, some general male arousal triggers might really be able to turn them on. Like, really turn them on, which means you're going to want to try them, like, yesterday.

First thing's first, though. It's important to remember that "man" doesn't necessarily = penis. While there are some general penis-related male arousal triggers, there are even more spots that can be found on all body types. This is because many erogenous areas on the body your brain deems pleasurable to the touch are universal. And these universal hotspots are kind of like arousal shortcuts. If you find your partner's e-zones, "You can take them from zero to Oh my god! In a matter of seconds."

Granted, you could argue that any zone on someone's body could be an arousal trigger if treated appropriately, but there is evidence that some specific areas are worth paying more attention to than others when it comes to pleasure. That's because some of these spots are full of nerve-endings (like your ears), while others are hot because they're so often easily overlooked (when was the last time you kissed the front of your partner's neck?).

And even though many people have similar erogenous zones and arousal triggers, note that everyone is different, so what makes your toes curl might not do the job for your partner, and vice versa. That's what makes discovering male arousal triggers so much fun. It's like unearthing a tactile treasure that your partner might not have even known about, which just makes it even hotter.

Yup, It's Time We Discuss Erogenous Zones or hotspots;

1. The Foreskin

Some people are circumcised (which is when the foreskin of the penis is cut off) and some people aren't, and neither is better than the other. But for those who are uncircumcised, there's a benefit: The foreskin amounts to around 15 square inches of bonus e-zone. The foreskin is packed with nerve endings, and stimulating the thin skin in this area lends a highly pleasurable experience. There's also sensitivity on both the outside and inside surfaces of the foreskin.

Use your hand to move the foreskin up and down over the head of the penis itself. During oral, you can also focus on it by using a combo of your hand, tongue, and lips. Because of the sensitivity on both the outside and inside of the foreskin, a rolling motion on the foreskin during sex can also be quite pleasurable.

2. Lower Stomach

Another nerve-filled area is the lower stomach, which becomes more and more concentrated closer to the genital area. Give the area right below their belly button but above their pubic bone or genitals some extra love to show them your affection and attention.

Teasing and stimulating this area can feel very pleasurable through kissing, gentle biting, and temperature play. You can even experiment with some light pressure play, but be careful it's best to try (pressure play) with an empty bladder.

3. Inner Arms

The thin, soft skin of the inner arms makes this area ultra-sensitive. Think about it, how often do you really give attention to your inner arms?

While most of these erogenous zones can be stimulated through kissing or your tongue, the light, controlled movement of your fingers is especially great for inner arms. Stroke the skin from just inside their inner shoulder and move gently down to the inner elbow. If you and your partner are both into BDSM and have spoken about trying it out, pulling this move when your partner has their arms tied up (either in a fixed T-shape or just with their wrists above their head), can be really sexy too.

4. Inner Wrist

Moving down the arm, stimulating the sensitive, thin skin of the inner wrist can also be incredibly pleasurable for your partner. Not only that, but feeling your partner's heart rate increase as you get closer to their pulse point can be both a turn-on and extremely empowering.

The inner wrist is a great erogenous zone you can stimulate while both of you are in public (in a non-gross) way. Simply stroking or kissing your partner's inner wrist is a great way to show that you're feeling sensual, and it's just a pretty sweet move overall.

5. Palm of Their Hands and Fingertips

Hands are actually some of the most sensitive and responsive areas of the body. This area is full of nerve-endings, a fact you probably already know if you've ever been bodied by a teensy paper-cut that somehow feels like someone cut your whole finger off.

Take your partner's palm in your hand and gently trace along the edges and lines of their palm with your fingertips. Then, turn it up by kissing his palms and fingertips, or gently taking one finger into your mouth to suck, swirling your tongue around their finger and moving your lips along its length.

6. Behind the Knee

Not only is the skin thin and sensitive, but it's also nerve-packed. Plus it gets points for being highly overlooked because truly, have you ever considered paying extra attention to the under-knee area? I didn't at first either.

The area behind the knee can be a super versatile erogenous zone as it can be teased without being gross in public, but also focused on during sex when you know you're back in private. Try gently running your fingers over the area, or engaging with this bodily real estate during penetrative sex with touching, stroking, or dialing the intensity up a bit by applying pressure.

7. Anus

While you might've heard about the prostate being wowza-levels pleasurable for those with penises, even without the prostate, backdoor play can still be something pleasurable you engage in with your partner. There are tons of nerve endings in the anal region, and once you've discussed and okay-ed anal play, it can be a really hot experience for you both. Remember, as with all things butt play, the importance of lube, patience, and ongoing consent cannot be stressed enough. The anus doesn't self-lubricate like a vagina, so lots of lube is a must for this situation.

For those who want to explore anal play but aren't sure if they want to give or receive anal penetration quite yet, don't worry, you can absolutely stimulate the anus without penetration. I recommend starting with massaging your partner's buttocks. Stroke the entire area and place your hands on the folds where the legs and buttocks meet, then slide your fingers across the fold from the inner thigh to the outer area, before starting to caress the outside of the anus.

After that, if you and your partner have spoken about anal penetration just yet, don't worry, you may definitely stimulate the anus without penetration. I propose beginning with rubbing your partner's buttocks. Stroke the whole region and lay your hands on the folds where the legs and buttocks meet, then run your fingers over the fold from the inner thigh to the outside area, before commencing to caress the outside of the anus.

After that, if you and your partner have discussed about anal penetration as something you both want to accomplish, then that's when you may start thinking about going towards penetration with either your (well-lubed) finger or toy.

8. Outer Thighs

Some of the finest erogenous zones are locations we may innocently caress in regular life, and the thighs are an outstanding example. Thighs are comparable to the groin or inner thigh, but considerably less personal, so you may make contact with the region in public without a hitch.

Try softly stroking or squeezing and gently massaging the region while sitting close to your spouse. Specifically, zone in on the spot between their knees and halfway up the leg, since this teasing movement will make them desire more. When you are in private, you may, of course, cover this region with soft licks, kisses, and even little bites, if that's something you're both like.

9. Inner Thighs

Since the inner thigh is so near to the penis, even without the sense of contact, simply being in that location is guaranteed to make your partner anticipate what's next.

Take your time to kiss and tongue your partner's inner thigh before going to contact their penis while doing oral. Tease and explore with your lips, moving from soft fluttering kisses to stronger sucking.

10. Groin

Similar to the inner thighs, this region is so near to the genitals that having you tease your partner in this area may be equally irritating and fulfilling. To really tease your partner, have them keep their underwear on while you run your fingers over the area slowly, before eventually moving to touch the groin, aka where your abdomen transitions into the lower body and legs, is packed with nerve endings, and it just gets bonus points for being adjacent to the genitals.

Once undressed, go ahead to kissing and stroking the region, and particularly doing so if you're performing oral, as this may make things even more personal.

11. Ears

Ears are susceptible to touch since there are hundreds of feeling receptors throughout the inside and outside of the ear.
Suck the top part of your partner's ear and then run your tongue along the inside. The beauty of ear play is that when you're that up close and personal, your hands are also free to roam the rest of their body.

12. Ribs

Anywhere of the body that has thinner skin is going to have higher sensitivity to sensation and more chance of blood flow during arousal. The ribs are one of these locations, and since they're normally covered up by clothes, there's a touch of taboo involved.
In case your partner is ticklish, try the region out first with a teasing touch, softly running your hands and fingers along the sides of their body or leaving a small breadcrumb trail of kisses or light nibbles on their ribcage.

13. Armpits

Another sensitive place that may also be ticklish, armpits are frequently disregarded but can still be very delightful for folks. While the pits don't have any particular nerve endings, they may nonetheless be incredibly intimate due to their under-serviced position as an erogenous zone.
Go for some sucking, licking, or mild, teasing caressing say. Armpits may also be mutually advantageous locations to pay attention to

during sex because they release smell is wonderful for feeling primal when you're going hot and heavy.

14. Fingers

It's Time We Revive the Hand Job. What better place to start than the receptor sites for perceiving touch? Just because you utilize them and they're well, there, in every sex act doesn't mean they can't profit from having the spotlight focused upon them as well.

Go on with rubbing their fingers (because how nice is that massage part during a manicure, right?), kissing your partner's finger pads softly, sliding your teeth down the side of them lightly, or placing them in your mouth and drawing them out slowly. All the better if you turn up the eye contact during the last part.

15. Their Beard

If your partner has facial hair, you can really work it to your advantage. Think about how sexy it feels when someone runs their fingers through your hair. For some reason, we seldom think of someone's beard being the same way, terrible, isn't it?

Start at the base of your partner's neck and trace your fingers up slowly through their beard, eventually running over their scalp. This trick feels so good that it won't be long before their fingers are eventually entangled in your hair as well.

16. The Base of the Shaft

The penis really extends farther into the body than you may think at first look, which means it's a fantastic spot to experiment with pressure and improve blood flow.

Using your fingers, find the base of the penis and explore with pressure. At the base of the penis, explore putting pressure around the shaft with your index finger and thumb in an 'ok' symbol, pushing back towards the body. While your fingers are getting to work, use your other free hand or mouth to stimulate the head of your partner's penis.

17. The Back of Their Neck

This is a hot location because of the numerous nerve endings there. It'll also provide you some under-utilized hot spot spots since it's generally disregarded when it comes to getting it on.
Try licking a path right below your partner's hairline, down their neck, and down the sides. You may also start with gentle, seductive kisses, progressively relaxing your tongue to turn up any sensitivity.

18. Their Hair

You know how lovely it feels when someone plays with your hair? The same thing happens for males, you all. Men have nerve endings on their scalp that are linked to the rest of their body, and when their hair is gently tugged when they are kissed or embraced, it transmits stimulation to the rest of their body.
While kissing, try sliding the tips of your fingers through your man's hair, lightly over their scalp, then a little firmer with a pull. If they respond with little grunts and pleasure sighs, pull harder, then release go before they want you to. This gentle tease will drive them really mad.

19. Their Toes

Shrimping anyone? Yes, this is what it's called when you suck on your partner's toes(or they suck on yours). This is so erotic because feet are a nonconventional hotbed of sensation just waiting for some stimulation.
During sexy foreplay, move your kisses teasingly down their body until you're all the way down at their feet. Suck on your partner's

toes or even gently biting each little piggie. Just maybe have them take a shower first.

20. Between Their Toes

You've already had their toes in your mouth, so while you're there, give additional attention to the region between the toes. The skin between our toes is incredibly sensitive and thin, making this location an undervalued erogenous zone to hone in on.

Use your pinkie, not a thumb or index finger, to caress the region between the toes. Odds are, your partner's never once been touched there, and they'll be both excited and shocked when you strike this ignored place. Try mixing up the pressure, like with your fingernail, to see what takes your boyfriend over the brink.

21. The Bottom of Their Feet

The bottoms of the feet tend to receive the most attention during foot massages and pedicures, and for good reason. This region is covered with pressure points and arousal zones, which makes the arches a particularly popular location individuals want to be stroked, no matter their gender or sexual inclinations.

Okay, so although this is a highly sensual location to touch, it also has big tickle potential, so you'll want to avoid quick motions that flit down the skin. You want them groaning, not giggling. So instead, use a delicate, calm, continuous stroke with the tips of your fingers. Try changing up the pressure to really get the blood flowing.

22. The Dip under Their Ankle

Yes, the place that usually gets screwed up when you wear new shoes! Between your man's heel and ankle lies a fingertip-size pressure spot that carries huge passion potential. This region is related to the sex organs and squeezing it releases energy, giving sensations of pleasure.

While in reverse cowgirl, grip your partner's feet and pulse each pressure point in sync with your thrusts. Try this soon before your guy is about to climax to truly blow their head.

23. The Prostate

This is essentially how to Find a Guy's G-Spot. The most undervalued feature of a penis-physique. The prostate gland is a vast erogenous zone. If correctly aroused, this may deliver immense pleasure to your lover. Think of this as your partner's penis-having clitoris, it's their most sensitive region.

Run a greased finger around your partner's anus to begin. This stimulation by itself may be plenty, but if they're down for more, and after the muscles have had a chance to relax, enter your index finger approximately two inches within, where you should be able to feel the prostate. Bend your finger up toward their abdomen and massage it.

24. Their Imagination

Okay, so maybe this isn't a real item you can touch, but trust: You can totally excite your partner's thoughts, and it's hot as hell. Let them have some time to ponder your touch before your fingers reach their flesh. The greatest tease.

Whisper in their ear quietly and tell them all the things you are going to do without touching a hair on their body. No clue WTF to say? Just act like you're sexting and say those things.

25. Their Butt Cheek

Ah, the "sweet spot" of the body. Your partner's going to be extremely sensitive here, striking their butt cheek, even softly, tends to excite the entire region. Think of it as a gentle vibration spreading through your man's insides.

If your partner is amenable to a little spanky play, this is fantastic to do when they're on top of you in any variant of missionary. Squeeze their booty when they're hitting precisely the right place, or give them a short swat if you're both into it. Don't be scared to grip or stroke there.

26. The Philtrum

The philtrum, or the little groove above your lips, has long been regarded as an erogenous zone. In fact the name itself, "philtrum," translates from the Latin phrase for "love potion."

To stimulate your partner's philtrum, lay a very delicate kiss on this spot immediately before moving your tongue down the groove to meet their top lip.

27. The Raphe

The raphe is the separating line that goes across the center of a penis-genitalia.This line travels from the anus to the apex of the penis, down across the perineum, scrotum, and shaft.

Use your tongue to draw along the line. To take things a step further, and also integrate a lubed-up bullet vibrator to trace down the line as well as you breathe, lick, and suck in combination with the vibrator.

28. Bottom Lips

Lips in general are one of the most sensitive areas of the body. Take your time when kissing, there's a reason nibbling and variety in pressure may send you over the edge when done right.

Go forward with nipping your man's bottom lip and potentially even going for a harsher bite (if they look open to it) (if they seem receptive to it). The sensations of transitioning from a soft kiss to some teeth may startle your spouse and thrill their brain.

29. Those V-Lines

Besides being sexy and entertaining for you to look at, the V-zone is a source of pleasure for your boyfriend. Not only is it a turn-on that your partner gets front-row seats to see you excite them, but it's a simple pit stop to make on the journey to bone-town.
Have your partner lay on their back while you get on top, straddle style. Starting at their belly button, use your fingertips and nails to draw a line down from their happy trail stopping before you touch their crotch. Then reverse your steps, but use your tongue to draw a V shape from their hips to directly above their penis. Repeat as desired and drag it out to truly tease them.

30. The Outside of Their Lower Lip

You know that place between the lower lip and the chin where you generally break out? Yeah, the one that one hair constantly shoots out of? That's an erogenous zone. That this little, delicate curvature is really filled with exceptionally sensitive nerve receptors.
Suck your partner's lower lip into your mouth the next time you're making out and use the tip of your tongue to rub this under-lip region. That motion stimulates the whole erogenous zone in a teasing way, which will put your partner on the erotic edge. And by keeping their lower lip inside yours, you magnify the sensation. It'll feel as if electric currents are shooting from their mouth straight to their member.

31. The Front of Their Neck

I bet you've never thought of your partner's Adam's apple as an erogenous zone, huh? In reality, the sexy area isn't one to skip when stimulating the body, especially because the attraction to throat fruit stems from how the thyroid (just below the Adam's apple) is closely linked to the sex organs, according to ancient Chinese medicine.

Have your spouse lay on their back and softly lick their Adam's apple. Keep your tongue flat and light, and don't apply too much pressure. Simply massage the region with large circular strokes to ensure you're reaching the T-spot of the thyroid.

32. Their Nipples

Wait, Can We Discuss Nipple-Only Orgasms? Oh yes. While all nipples are basically the same, males could feel higher nipple sensitivity because they aren't normally as accustomed to having them handled. For a lot of guys, their nipples are new terrain, an erogenous zone they haven't played with.

Have your spouse lay back and gently lick from their areola inward (like an ice-cream cone), but never really contact your tongue to their nip. Get closer and closer till you flick their nipple with your tongue and then softly bite it. If you want to be very extra, you can suck on an ice cube prior for greater feeling.

33. The Perineum

The perineum, which is the area of skin positioned between a penis-testicles haver's and anus is just above the prostate gland. And this whole area has major orgasmic power. In fact, a few light strokes here will send your lover to the verge.

Press your knuckles lightly into this place and start rubbing. Right as your partner's ready to climax, press your knuckles a bit deeper to lengthen the pyrotechnics.

34. The Shaft

This sex organ is, unsurprisingly, a big element of sex for males. And although you may have perfected the regular handy and blow job, try to liven things up with something entirely unexplored like a reverse finger job.

Make two tight rings around your partner's penis with your thumb and index finger (like you're making the okay hand sign), stacking them one on top of the other in the center of the shaft. Twist the rings in opposing directions going from the center to the top with one hand, and the middle to the base of the shaft with the other hand, both at the same time. It's sort of like patting your head and massaging your tummy at the same time, but if you can master the torrid twist, your spouse will undoubtedly appreciate you. Remember to use lubrication however.

35. The Head of the Penis

As the most sensitive portion of the penis, the head may be a difficult location to dominate. It may be tough to obtain the exact degree of pressure to send your lover flying into pleasure without recoiling in sensory overload.

Give your guy a lipstick blow job, aka where you brush your closed but relaxed lips across the head of their penis like you're applying lipstick. Hold their shaft with your fingers, but not in a fist (avoid holding their penis like a microphone, but do approach it with the same naïve confidence of a terrible stand-up performance) (avoid holding their penis like a microphone, but do approach it with the same blind confidence of a mediocre stand-up act). Varying the sensations by expanding your lips a little and massaging the penis head between them.

36. The Seam of Their Testicles

You know how socks usually have a seam in them? Well, your partner's penis has one that divides their testicles that stops them from forming one enormous testilump. It's a nerve-rich pleasure trail that runs top to bottom along the scrotum and is vastly under-appreciated.

Cradle your partner's balls with one hand while softly pushing the first two fingers of your other hand into the top of the crease (near to where the testicles attach to the base of his penis) (close to where the testicles connect to the base of his penis). Then trail downward with your fingertips until you reach the bottom of the scrotum. Don't forget to be gentle, that is extremely important, you are aiming for pleasure and not pain.

37. Their Frenulum

The F-spot is the tiny nubbin of skin below the crown of the penis that links the head to the shaft. It's commonly neglected since it's part of the undercarriage, but there's really a bundle of nerves at this location that when touched set off an astounding chain reaction of pleasure.

The next time you're going down on your spouse, keep their penis firmly with one hand while truly giving their crown your all. Each time you loop your tongue around to the frenulum, flick it a few times with your tongue stiffened, and then relax and go back to licking the crown.

38. Their Lower Back

If you're searching for a method to turn your spouse's TF on without even getting their trousers down, look no further. The pudendal nerve that stimulates all the parts of the groin is situated here, near the bottom of the spinal cord.

Have your spouse lie on their stomach with their shirt off and their arms by their side. Hot tip: Keep their trousers on, but pull them down a few inches for a thrilling never-nude sensation. Lightly move your fingertips down over their lower back, pausing before you contact butt cheek.

39. Their Earlobes

We have discussed the ears, but this delicate tiny pocket of flesh needs its own section since it's so sexy. Just think about how jumpy you become when someone whispers in your ear. Now take that experience to the next level by integrating earlobe nibbles and below-the-belt multitasking.

Start by kissing your lover across their shoulder, up their neck, and pausing immediately before you contact their ear. Do this on both sides, since asymmetry is for the lazy. When they get real squirmy, start kissing their earlobes, then play around with gentle nibbles, tongue, etc. If you want to start talking nasty, now's the moment. But be warned: Only utilize this maneuver if you want a quickie since very few individuals can stay long in bed when earlobes are integrated.

Chapter 6: How to Initiate Sex with Your Man and Signal Your Desire Subtly

There's something reassuring about having your lover be the one to initiate sex first. When your spouse initiates love making it gives you the assurance that he's in the mood and makes you feel wanted. However, if your spouse is the sole one initiating sex, it may lead you to feel embarrassed or uncomfortable when you are the one who wants to address the matter. You may think, "Should women initiate sex?"

This may cause many wives and girlfriends feel irritated and go without sex due to not wanting to be the one to make the approach. However, Women initiating sex works wonders.

How to Please Your Man in the Bedroom

Going without sex merely because you aren't sure how to make the move might make you irritated and upset with your lover. But remember, he is not a mind reader. Making physical intercourse with your partner shouldn't be something you should be ashamed or apprehensive about. From subtle to in-your-face ques. You want to make sure that your partner stays content with you in a sexual way? You want to satisfy his sexual desire and make sure that his every demand is met? You want to learn how to make love to your spouse and how to give him one of the finest orgasms of his life? Read on girl.

In order to please your partner effectively, you need to understand certain sex advice for women. That is the only way that you are going to obtain the guidance and assistance that you need to offer him the sort of pleasure that he is yearning for. Without learning these principles, you may expect your sex life to stay subpar. If you don't want that, then now is the moment for you to expand your mind and allow these sex tips for women to pleasure a guy to his utmost climax potential, take you away.

First of all, tease your guy. It is a frequent misperception that women have that men dislike a tease. Men truly love to be played with and fooled with as long as they are getting pleasure out of it at the end. Feel free to tease him since this will make him desire you terribly. The more he desires you and the more you reject his approaches, then the more aroused he gets. When he is asking for you and desiring you in the worst manner, then when you do eventually touch him, sparks will fly. Creating sexual tension and offering him release afterwards is the greatest approach to pleasure your partner.

To make love to your spouse the proper manner, this implies that you really have to make love to him. Even if the missionary position is your typical go-to staple, you need to mix things up. Show your lover how much you adore him and how attractive you think he is.

Your man will feel desired and he will feel more pleasure if you take the reins in the bedroom. Don't be afraid to unleash the naughty girl within you. Your boyfriend wants to see this side of you.

Another sex tip to pleasure him in the greatest manner possible is to employ more oral sex. You may use oral sex on him as a prologue to sex or you can use it as the primary event. No matter which one you select, just make sure you deliver it to him. Men adore this type of stimulation and the more you offer it to him, the closer the two of you will get. As well, he would want to return the pleasure and the experience for you and that is always excellent.

Another technique to make love to your spouse and to pleasure him to his greatest capacity is to apply as much stimulation on him as you can. Of course, you stimulate his penis during intercourse or oral, but the male orgasm is a lot more in depth than that. This is something that a lot of ladies would frequently disregard. Your lover wants more pleasure than what you are only offering to him. He wants to hear you moan and groan in the bedroom and he wants to feel you be harsh with him. He wants those nails to sink deep in his back. By providing him more stimulation, you contribute more to his orgasm and consequently, you make it stronger and considerably more powerful.

Use these sex tips for women on your man tonight so you can show him that you are an incredible lover in the bedroom and that you do have a few tricks up your sleeve that he hasn't seen before. You can and you will blow him away tonight.

When you have little sexual confidence in the bedroom, more than only your sex life suffers. You aren't taking charge of your femininity and the sexual power that you can possess. Find out what you can do, beginning now, to dramatically improve the intimate connection you have with your man and yourself from this chapter. We're looking at techniques on how to make love to your man in a way that he will never forget.

1. Create a Buildup

If you want to make the first move for a physical connection but aren't sure where to begin, don't be frightened. You don't have to be extremely forward or do anything outside of your comfort zone to grab his attention. Letting your partner know you're in the mood doesn't mean pouncing on him as soon as he enters through the front door.

Initiating sex is all about establishing a buildup. Plan a romantic evening with wine and light some candles. Or be spontaneous and start by giving him a massage or cuddling on the sofa while you watch television. He will get the hint.

2. Send a Lewd Text

If you're bashful about verbalizing your wants, why not SMS it to your man? Many couples share sexy messages and photographs back and forth, however, exchanging nude photos is not always secure.

There are lots of ways to send a tempting picture without baring it all. For example, you may snap a photo of your finest underwear set out on the bed. Typing out your wishes is often a terrific method to attract his attention. A simple statement suggesting that you can't wait for him to come home followed up with a funny but suggestive wink will deliver the message loud and clear.

If you do send a nude image to your guy, make careful to keep your face out of it. Not only does it provide you a feeling of safety, but it also increases your man anticipation.

3. Create a Filthy Code Word

If you're timid about starting sex but still want your partner to know you're liking the idea, you may set up a wicked code word in advance. Choose a term or phrase that is inoffensive. Take the sentence "I have to wash my hair" for example. This remark may be stated in front of your children or out in public allowing only you and your spouse to know what it actually means. This feeling of wicked mystery promotes closeness and enhances excitement between you and your companion. This way, he knows precisely what you want when you go back home.

4. Go Totally Physical

Men don't always pick up on subtle clues, particularly when it comes to sex. You may spend your entire day dropping subtle indications that you want to go to the bedroom with no beneficial effects. In your opinion, he's rejecting your approaches, in his mind no offer was ever made. To be straightforward, when it comes to establishing sexual intimacy with your man, nuance is not your friend.

If you want to put the offer out there but are too bashful to articulate it, consider taking the physical approach. Start by kissing him or sitting on his lap. Get close together while watching a movie and move your hand along the essential portions of his body. He'll know what you're wanting.

5. Dress up and Role-play

Nothing screams 'Take me now' like getting up for the occasion. Slip on your sexiest negligee and stroll into your bedroom. You don't even have to strut if you don't want to. Just walk in looking stunning in your corset or baby doll chemise and he'll know just what you're seeking.

If you're feeling daring you can even throw roleplay into the mix. Dress up in a costume, such as a policewoman or a cheerleader, and roleplay as soon as you have your spouse alone.

6. Unexpected Initiation

One technique to make physical relations with your spouse is by starting at a moment that is unexpected for you as a pair. Instead of sticking to the old standard of making love before night, try passionately kissing him in the morning before work, dropping in on him in the shower, or making a move while you're out in the vehicle. The spontaneity of this move will assist make the moment seem heightened because it is out of the norm for you both. This will help you both to let loose and really shed your inhibitions.

7. Reminisce

Reminiscing is a great way to start intimacy with your man and get your blood flowing without coming right out and telling him what you want. Start out by casually asking whether he recalls "such and such" a time together and progressively progresses towards the more sexual component of the narrative. Think back on especially heated occasions or hazardous activity your spouse liked. This is a sort of verbal foreplay that is aimed to get him thinking about sex and envisioning what it feels like to be intimate with you. Once you start talking, the tale will take care of the rest.

8. Just Ask

Don't forget that being direct is always an option. You do not have to coax your spouse into bed with you by playing the "remember when" game or by sending filthy photographs or ideas. Instead, why not approach him and say "I'm heading to the bedroom, like to join me?" or "Wanna do it?" Or just start kissing him in a manner that implies this is not a normal peck of love. If he thinks that you almost never initiate affection, this is the perfect solution.
Men find it exciting when a woman displays confidence and asks for what she wants. Being direct means spending less time coming up with a way to seduce your husband and more time alone together.

9. Schedule it

To spice up your sex life and keep your spouse reminded of the closeness you both have, you could arrange your sex.
People are frequently caught up in their hectic lives and occasionally, it gets tough to maintain the closeness levels intact. In

this scenario, if you both arrange sex time as well as days, it will enhance your relationship. It could appear forced in the beginning, but it will truly do wonders in establishing affection.

10. Talk About it

Talk about sex in your free time. So, this will remind your husband of the fantastic sensation and as the intensity of the talk rises, he will undoubtedly feel turned on and more inclined towards you.
You may start a random sex chat, about any one occasion you both greatly loved that is imprinted in your mind or inquire about his likes and dislikes.

11. Take Turns

If you wonder how to begin sex with your man where you both play an equal role, taking turns is the finest deal. In order to not let sex fade away from your lives, you both must make efforts to establish a strong physical bond. You can do so by taking the responsibility alternatively. This means that if you initiated sex the last time, it will be your husband's turn to do so the next time.

12. Use Positive Affirmations

Positive affirmations for sex will reach deep into your man's subconscious mind and motivate him to act. Affirmations are used to help influence your mind and replace old or negative beliefs with new ones and affirmations for sex will activate the areas of the brain that make him feel happy and fulfilled.

13. Try Shower Sex

If you wonder how to initiate sex with your spouse that looks like a scene from a sassy movie then shower sex is your answer.

Shower sex is one of the creative ways to initiate lovemaking and looks something straight out of the movie. So, try some sexy positions like the Chairperson, Standing Doggy, etc. to turn up the heat. Make sure you have certain guidelines in mind like utilizing an anti-slip mat and using a shower-friendly lubrication to prevent any type of mishap or difficulties.

14. Be a Masseuse

Massages may work wonders to turn your hubby on. Erotic massages are not only soothing and assist relieve stress but also helps boost sexual pleasure. Ensure to establish the atmosphere first. For the first 15-20 minutes, it should be a typical massage and then, gently begin to rub and play with their genital region. Give them the time and mental space to receive you.

15. Look Different

Change your look dramatically. With spouses, one of the issues with long-term relationships is that we become too comfortable with them and are used to seeing them in their roughest state. So, for a change, dress differently and surprise them.

16. Use Bodily Language

If you don't desire to be too explicit about your urge for sex but need to advise him, you may use different body language cues to let him know. For instance, you may smile at him, shift your shoulders towards him, brush your fingers on his palms, and massage his knee and so forth.

17. Be Attentive of Hygienes

Perfect sex begins with great hygiene. You must maintain good hygiene to turn your man on. Everyone has ideas about the cleanliness levels but the essentials apply to everyone. Some advice for sexual hygiene are that you should maintain a check on your intimate regions for any anomalies, select loser fitting for undergarments and replace the undergarment everyday.

18. Sleep Nude

A physical contact between husband and wife helps develop the entire bond. You may opt to sleep nude to turn your hubby on. Once he sees you without clothing next to himself, he is bound to make a move, if not immediately, then surely after a time.

19. Flash

Flash yourself in front of your partner and he is likely to be taken aback and be turned on. This is a terrific technique of flirting with him and telling him what he is missing at the time.

20. Try the no Panties Game

You can choose to take off your panties when you both go out for dinner. Discreetly remove them and let him know when he is waiting outside the washroom for you. He is sure to be on fire till the time you both get back home.

If you wish to create physical relations with your spouse, make it known. Initiating sex should never be left completely to one partner. Practice these methods for initiating sex in your relationship and he'll receive the message loud and clear.

Chapter 7: How Do Men Feel After Sex?

Sex is an act of incredible intimacy that can make you experience different things. Generally, your body goes through certain phases before you achieve a climax. It is usual not to pay attention to how your body responds after sex due to weariness or simply enjoying the moment. You may feel some aspects that may seem a bit unusual, but it is crucial to realize that sexual intimacy encompasses the whole body. This chapter will throw light on what occurs after sex and help you understand how your man feels.

What Happens After Sex?

The sexual response cycle is a hypothesis that describes how the body feels and reacts towards sexual closeness. There are four phases of this cycle: the excitation phase, the plateau, the orgasm, and the resolution phase. During these phases of physical closeness, sexual arousal tends to peak and concludes with the release. You can experience muscle contractions as your body releases all the pent up sexual tension while it reaches a climax. Men experience a tightening and release at the base of the penis while they ejaculate.
Now that all the energy has been released, their body slowly returns to pre-sex state. Their heart rate will steadily return back to normal during this period, and respiration will decrease down. The tightened muscles will relax as the male sex organs recover to their natural size, color, and form. They can feel tired, calm, or satisfied.

However, it is important to note that this cycle is a way to classify the human response towards sex. In reality, every guy is different; hence, they can experience sex and its aftermath differently.

Stages of an Orgasm

1. Excitement Stage

The heart rate of an individual increases while the muscles become tense. This characterizes a healthy blood flow to the genitals.

2. Plateau Stage

While the muscles continue to tighten, the testicles begin sensing a pull.

3. Orgasm Stage

The muscles of the male genital penis contract and retract. Their body gets flushed and crimson. With penis, they end up ejaculating.

4. Resolution Stage

The tight muscles in the body begin returning to their former condition, blood pressure lowers and heart rate gradually calms down.

How Your Man Does Feels After Sex

What goes on in a man's mind after sex? Men and women are said to reflect a different performance after sexual intercourse. In some situations, however, men match them. "Men just want to sleep after sex" is virtually always heard. You will see that this is not totally correct. Prejudice may disguise the truth.

1. They Feel fatigued

Lack of interest? The sex was too good? Neither question can be addressed if you wind up fatigued after sex. Research has demonstrated that physical activity during sex and after an orgasm depletes the muscle glycogen (the major muscle fuel) (the predominant muscle fuel). That is why many men end up as zombies, and they only want to sleep. The only thing they are merely seeking for is their own mattresses or a suitable area to stop and relax a little after all the energy used in their intense session. ZZZ… Sleep and repose.

2. They Believe They Desire More Sex

Some express that they can last all night. They claim they are more active than ever, and they look forward to doing it again. It is evident that at least a few minutes are required in order to return to the action. However, it is important to remember that if this behavior is persistent, he could suffer from an addiction. In such instances, it relies not just on the guy and his sexual urges. Both you and the other person should desire the same.

3. They Feel Sad

Although it sounds like a paradox, it is more widespread than most people think. There is even a term "post-coital dysphoria". This is a disorder that causes feeling sad or anxious, for no apparent reason, after having sex. In situations such as this, consult your health care provider to determine the specifics of the test. Keep calm, it is not the end of the world. There are numerous approaches to properly treat people with this illness.

4. They Feel they Want to Embrace and Kiss

It is often considered that this is for ladies. However, guys also desire and demand hugs and kisses. These positive gestures may reflect satisfaction after sexual intercourse. Or maybe a wish for another round. And why not? It might be the beginning of a new session.
Typically, this condition arises in a partnership of mutual trust. Touching, holding, and caressing are additional methods to show your affection for your mate. Nevertheless, some people are too shy to express their emotions.

5. They Feel Proud of Themselves

Some are very proud of themselves after having sex. They feel they are too good to have intercourse. And who knows, maybe your spouse has also had this experience. Imagine this. Aren't you a little jealous of this? Obviously. Many would have wanted to be in that situation.
Having sex is one of the joys of life. For some, the fact that reaching orgasm is enough, while for others this is more than just climax. What it means to have sex can vary greatly from one person to the next. As you can see, there are plenty of feelings and emotions behind what is being said.

What Does a Man Thinks About After Having Sex With You?

Lying down with your partner after making love to them feels great. But as males would have it, their brains spin around with various notions shortly after having sex. Many guys are anxious about whether their spouse enjoys having sex with them. Or if they were good enough in bed. Let's take a look as we break down what guys generally think after you have sex with them. These hot questions are likely to get you captivated and make you startled as a woman.

Did she Enjoy it?

Men would want to receive feedback from their woman love, on whether they loved having sex with them or not. Every man wants to know whether their girlfriend fully enjoyed the time, just like them. They want to check whether their spouse is enthusiastic to proceed for round 2.

Did she Orgasm?

The big-O! Every male is the most dubious about orgasms and pleasure. Since typically, males tend to climax sooner than women, they prefer to imagine their partner has climaxed as well. But most of the time, this isn't the case. It wounds a man's ego to know their partner hasn't attained their climax.

Should I Stay?

Those men who engage in casual or hookup sex with their partners are often left wondering whether they should stay after having sex or not. Since having sex is the main priority in casual relationships, staying after sex is something many women might not like or maybe can get too awkward.

Did I Finish Too Fast?

Every guy who comes within a matter of minutes or even seconds thinks this. They might feel embarrassed over orgasming this early, compared to their partner.

Was I the Greatest she Ever had?

To know that your spouse had the finest sex with you, is an achievement for many males. They definitely adore the fact that their spouse believes they had the finest sex with them. Men further want to know what made them distinct from all the other males their spouse had sex with.

What's after this?

Ladies, males either think about having round 2 or are busy thinking about when to take you out for the next date. After having sex, males tend to worry about the future with the woman they just made love to, unless it's not a casual relationship. If it's the latter, guys consider quietly fleeing the flat and getting the next cab to their house.

Conclusion

What a Man Wants Most From His Woman

It is thought that males are hardwired to be hunters. They need to obtain what they desire no matter what it takes. Successful hunters, who bring home the prey, are recognized as victors. Though today's men are more likely to merely order sandwiches, rather than hunt for wild boar for supper, there remains within them the basic need to win.

That is what they require from their women, they want and need to win. It is not essential for them to win in every debate and be always correct but they desire the sense of victory. If a male believes that his lady trusts him, it will make him feel like a winner. If a guy is regularly put down by his wife or spouse, then he would feel like he is a total loser. He may pretend that his woman's opinion isn't really important to him but deep down it does matter a lot.

Aside from that relentless urge to win, males also require space. Some women really push their guys away by asking that their partner spend so many hours with them. Men need to connect with their pals and speak about their victories together. They need time to enjoy sports, and other interests and hang out with their male pals. A clever woman would know when to let her guy have his own time, since it would often endear her more to him. Some ladies who are extremely demanding and possessive, and oblivious to their men's requirements of alone time, will only end up dissatisfied and unhappy.

Be your man's lover and friend at the same time. Make him feel that he can open up and chat to you about anything and anything without being judged and ridiculed. If your relationship is established on friendship, he absolutely would not do anything to ruin that friendship. If you can keep that relationship even after the wedding, then your marriage has a greater chance of survival.

Aside from these two essential wants; the drive to win and the need to have time for themselves, men also need to see their spouses taking care of themselves. Not that women would always have to appear like super models to keep their men happy, but spending the time and effort to look beautiful for their man is equally necessary. This will help men appreciate the time that wives spend on looking attractive exclusively for them.

A relationship is not a battle where you only offer the other person what he needs if he begins giving you what you desire. There is no space for this type of mentality in a healthy relationship. By being sensitive to your partner's needs your life together will be more meaningful and your marriage will develop stronger over the years.

50 percent of individuals divorce or split up from a fruitful partnership. Do not be another statistic. You Can Save Your Relationship. These are strong tactics that will help you to trust again and spark the fire and passion back into your relationship.

Printed in Great Britain
by Amazon

22794569R10046